INTRODUCTION

NOTES FOR PARENTS AND TEACHERS.

The Programmes of Study in English require a pupil to have knowledge in the areas of comprehension, spelling, punctuation and grammar. The material in these tests can be used to develop these skills.

The tests contain much of the work to be covered by the end of a child's primary career.

This material may ... the child for gramm...

There is no time lim... Many of the English ... are explained in the g...

GLOSSARY

Adjective:- a word which describes a noun.
e.g. a *wonderful* boy.

Adverb:- gives more information about a verb, adjective or other adverb.
e.g. he ran *quickly*.

Compound word:- a word made up from two or more other words.
e.g. coast and guard become *coastguard*.

Conjuction:- a word that connects sentences or parts of sentences. e.g. *but*, *because*.

Contraction:- two words shortened into one word by the use of an apostrophe.
e.g. he will becomes *he'll*.

Exclamation mark (!):- used to show strong emotions.

Homonyms:- words that are spelt differently and have different meanings but sound the same.
e.g. *flower* and *flour*.

Inverted commas (also known as quotation marks or speech marks):- used to show the exact words that have been spoken.

Noun:- the name of a person, place or thing.

Plural:- a word meaning more than one thing.
e.g. *foxes*.

Prefix:- one or more letters added to the beginning of a word to form a new word.
e.g. *MIS*place

Pronouns:- words that are used to replace nouns.
e.g. *it*, *he*.

Suffix:- one or more letters added to the end of a word to form a new word.
e.g. bliss*FUL*

Tense:- indicates when an action takes place. i.e. past, present or future.
e.g. he *ran*, he *runs*, he *will run*.

Their:- belonging to them
e.g. *their* teacher is ill.

There:- in a certain place.

To:- used alongside a verb.
e.g. *to* run, *to* write.

Too:- also, as well as, in addition to or meaning more than enough.
e.g. We went *too*. (also)
He ate *too* much.

Two:- meaning the number two, e.g. *two* boys

Verb:- a doing or action word.
e.g. *running*.

Were:- the plural of was.
e.g. He was at the shops.
They *were* at the shops.

Where:- relating to a place.
e.g. *Where* is it?

TEST ONE
&
TEST TWO

SCORE: TEST ONE _____

TEST TWO _____

TEST ONE

The following advertisement appeared in a local newspaper.

> **STANLEY BRAKE**
> **TOP CLASS DRIVING INSTRUCTOR**
>
> 1. Excellent success rate.
> 2. Competitive fees.
> 3. Door to door service.
> 4. Free introductory lesson.
> 5. Discount for young drivers.
> 6. Mornings, afternoons and evenings.
> 7. Seven days a week.
> 8. Lessons in your own car if requested.
> 9. Personal professional service.
> 10. Highly recommended.
>
> **Phone 123456.**

1 Which word above means the same as "reduction"? _____

2 Which word above means the same as "asked for"? _____

Ten points are given in the advertisement. Six are facts and four are claims.
Give three facts and three claims.

3 **4** **5**   Facts -   Numbers _____ _____ _____

6 **7** **8**   Claims -   Numbers _____ _____ _____

Which points in the advertisement suggest the following?

9 The instructor has good results.   Number _____

10 His teaching is well thought of.   Number _____

11 He doesn't charge as much as others.   Number _____

12 No charge is made for the first lesson.   Number _____

TEST ONE PAGE 1

Choose the best words to complete the passage so that it makes sense.
Choose from the words in **bold type**. Circle your chosen words.

13 - 18

BUDGERIGARS

Budgerigars are ideal pets for **(them, ones, those, family)** living in flats or single rooms. It is **(nice, advised, easy, best)** to buy a young budgie **(since, while, therefore, and)** it will be easier to train. Keep it in as big a cage as **(there are, needed, necessary, possible)** and away from draughts and **(dull, direct, morning, shining)** sunlight. It will take the budgie a few weeks to settle down in **(it's, your, its, some)** new home.

Complete each sentence by writing a word in the space.
Choose your answers from this list. Use each word only once.

dispute   humane   knowledge   loitered   temporary

optimist   patiently   potential   primitive   prominent

19 The motorist waited _____ in the traffic jam.
20 Several youths _____ at the corner with nothing to do.
21 Paul has good general _____ and will do well in the quiz.
22 An _____ always looks on the bright side.
23 Rubbing sticks together is a _____ way to light a fire.
24 The drivers had a _____ over who caused the accident.
25 The Prime Minister is a _____ member of the government.
26 The recaptured prisoners were not treated in a _____ way.
27 Lynne has a _____ job during the school holidays.
28 Your idea has a lot of _____ for making money.

TEST ONE PAGE 2

FAMOUS EXPLORERS

The date of birth, date of death, nationality and information about some explorers is given below. Use the information to answer the questions.

AMUNDSEN, Roald (1872-1928) Norwegian. First person to reach the South Pole. Arrived about a month before R.F.Scott.

BALBOA, Vasco Nunez de (1475-1517) Spanish. Discovered the Pacific Ocean.

COLUMBUS, Christopher (1451-1506) Italian. Discovered the West Indies. Explored the American coast.

COOK, James (1728-1779) English. Explored the seas around Australia. Killed by natives in Hawaii during exploration.

DIAZ, Bartholomew (died 1501) Portuguese. First person to sail round the Cape of Good Hope.

DRAKE, Francis (1540-1596) English. First Englishman to sail round the world. Fought against the Spanish Armada in 1588.

GAMA, Vasco Da (?1460-1524) Portuguese. Sailed round Africa to India.

LIVINGSTONE, David (1813-1873) Scottish. In 1840 he went to Africa. Discovered the Victoria Falls.

POLO, Marco (1254-1323) Venetian. Explored China and the Far East.

PEARY, Robert Edwin (1856-1920) American. First to reach the North Pole.

SCOTT, Robert Falcon (1868-1912) English of Scottish ancestors. Reached the South Pole after Amundsen. Died on return journey.

29) Which explorer was born first? _____

30) Which explorer died most recently? _____

31) What age was Sir Francis Drake when he fought the Spanish Armada? _____

32) Who died when he was 60 years old? _____

33) How many British explorers are mentioned? _____

34) How many explorers can we be certain died while exploring? _____

35) Why is there only one date given for Bartholomew Diaz? _____

36) Why is there a question mark beside one of Vasco Da Gama's dates? _____

37) When was the South Pole first reached? Circle one date.   1887   1898   1912   1928

38) When was the North Pole first reached? Circle one date.   1850   1867   1909   1922

39) Which explorer lived only during the 18th Century? _____

40) Can you suggest why David Livingstone named a waterfall the Victoria Falls? _____

The passage below is about the formation of stalagmites in caves.
The sentences are jumbled up. Unjumble them so that they make sense.

Label the sentences from 1 to 5.

41 - 45

STALAGMITES

Sentence order

Over a long period a pillar called a stalagmite is formed.　　　　　_____

When the drops evaporate the limestone particles are
left on the cave floor.　　　　　_____

The rainwater dripping from the ceiling of a cave carries
particles of limestone in it.　　　　　_____

A mound forms on the cave floor.　　　　　_____

When rain falls on a limestone area, it seeps through the
soil and becomes slightly acidic.　　　　　_____

Join each pair of sentences by using **conjunctions**. Choose from the list.
A conjunction may be used more than once. Write the new sentence on the line.

while   that   until   because   whether   but   although

Example.　　The boy did his homework. He was watching television.

　　　　　　The boy did his homework **while** he was watching television.

46　The police were called. There had been a serious accident.

_____

47　The choir boy tried to sing. He had a sore throat.

_____

48　We must stay indoors. The weather improves.

_____

49　Laura ran to the station. The train had just left.

_____

50　I know who did it. I saw what happened.

_____

TEST TWO

THE LOLLIPOP MAN

He stands by the roadside each morning
And again at a quarter to three,
Helping us safely cross over
When our parents aren't there to see.

He holds up his stick like a soldier
Warning enemies that they must wait,
So his troops can smartly march over
Moving swiftly so they are not late.

He greets each one smiling broadly
With a friendly word or two.
Without his laughter the world would be dull
And we'd all be left feeling blue.

But I'm the luckiest child of all
I never feel lonely nor sad,
For the lollipop man who stands on the street
Is Joe Fletcher, my own grandad!

Choose the **best word** or **phrase** each time. Underline your answers.

1 The poet believes that the lollipop man is

    shy and quiet   warm and friendly

    at war with enemies   always telling jokes

2 "Feeling blue" means to be -   happy   angry   sad   excited

3 The "enemies" are -   teachers   children   soldiers   cars

4 The lollipop man's job is -   detached   hazardous   dramatic   desperate

5 Children crossing busy roads without supervision are -   safe   fearless   in peril   bold

6 Who are the "troops" in the poem? _____

7 Why does the poet feel special? _____

Find words in the poem which mean the **OPPOSITE** to each of the following.

    Word from the poem   Word from the poem

e.g. early   <u>late</u>   **8** slowly _____

9 cheerful _____   **10** always _____

11 hostile _____   **12** most unfortunate _____

Write the **plural** of each of the following words.

13 boy   _____   14 child   _____
15 sheep   _____   16 box   _____
17 wolf   _____   18 goose   _____
19 potato   _____   20 soldier _____
21 deer   _____   22 wife   _____
23 chief   _____   24 shelf   _____
25 hero   _____   26 ox   _____

Insert the words **there** and **their** in the proper places in the sentences below.

27 The children left _____ coats in the corner over _____.

28 _____ mother had forgotten to make _____ dinner.

29 Are _____ too many holes in _____ old socks?

30 _____ books must be in _____ bags.

31 The teachers arrived in _____ classrooms before the children were _____.

32 _____ appears to be an elephant in _____ back garden.

33 _____ is nothing _____.

TEST TWO PAGE 2

FACT OR OPINION

Some statements are true and cannot be disproved. These are known as **FACTS**.
Example . Monday is the day after Sunday.

Other statements are ideas which may not be true. These are **OPINIONS**.
Example . Friday is the best day to shop.

Decide whether each statement below is a **FACT (F)** or an **OPINION (O)**.
Write **F** or **O** on the answer line.

34 Australia is a continent. _____

35 Chips taste better with vinegar. _____

36 Weeds are good for nothing. _____

37 Bad weather does not last forever in Britain. _____

38 Earthquakes can cause a lot of damage. _____

39 United is the best team in the world. _____

These words are going into the index of a book on musical instruments.
Write them in **alphabetical order.** The first one has been done for you.

piccolo   violin   trombone   harp   viola   piano   trumpet

harp   **40** _____   **41** _____   **42** _____
       43 _____   **44** _____   **45** _____

Put in **capital letters** and **full stops** where necessary. Write out the sentences.

46 my name is jimmy jones and i live in bristol

47 we went to london to visit buckingham palace

48 my favourite television programme is blue peter

49 the 26th december is boxing day

50 my uncle philip took me to see the film home alone

TEST TWO PAGE 3

TEST THREE
&
TEST FOUR

SCORE: TEST THREE _____

TEST FOUR _____

TEST THREE

Safety Notes and Operating Instructions
Floor Sander - Models 848 and 849.

N.B. Where possible a residual current circuit breaker (R.C.C.B.) should be used with this machine.

SAFETY NOTES.

A. Do not use the machine in damp conditions and do not expose it to rain.
B. Always wear goggles and a face mask.
C. Empty the dust collecting bag regularly, as the concoction of wood dust, paints, oils and varnishes is prone to combustion.
D. Wood dust is easily ignited :-
Do not smoke when using the machine.
Ensure all nails are removed or punched below the surface to avoid sparks.
Do not empty the dust on to an open fire.
E. If the machine fails to operate do not attempt to repair it. It should be returned to the distributor.

OPERATING INSTRUCTIONS.

A. Tilt the machine backwards and switch on.
B. Lower the machine gently on to the floor and always keep it moving to prevent gouges.
C. Close doors and open all windows to minimise the spread of dust.
D. Never use the machine without sandpaper fitted.
E. An edging sander, model E55, can be used to obtain very good results close to a skirting board.

---

1 What does R.C.C.B. stand for? _____

2 Why should you always wear goggles? _____

3 Why is wood dust very dangerous? _____

4 What should you not do if the machine fails to work? _____

5 Why should nails be punched below the surface or removed? _____

Choose one word which means **the same** or **almost the same** as the following.
Underline your answer.

6 concoction   paints   mixture   machine   sandpaper

7 combustion   varnish   dust   ignition   dampness

8 What must be fitted to the machine every time it is used? _____

9 How can you let dust out of a room? _____

10 What model number may be used to sand the edges of the floor? _____

Choose the best words to complete the passage so that it makes sense.
Choose from the words in **bold type**. Circle your chosen words.

11 - 16   **FIRST AID BOX**

Every house needs a first aid box which should be marked with a large red cross.

(Perhaps, Maybe, Really, Ideally) it should be kept in a place where

it is **(available, easy, ready, hard)** to get at, but yet out of reach of

small children. A **(strong, tight, slack, loose)** fitting lid which is

childproof is **(good, wrong, essential, bad)**. Antiseptic cream, bandages,

dressings and plasters should be **(seen, preserved, exposed, included)** in the

box. Scissors, tweezers and assorted safety pins **(and, are, is, include)**

useful items.

Find words which have **SIMILAR** meanings to the words in the list.
Choose your answers from the following words. Use each word only once.
The first one has been done for you.

| leave | beginning | emergency | fearful | strange | stubborn |
| accurately | mannerly | devour | idea | try | |

Example   abandon   ____leave____

17 cowardly   _____   **18** obstinate   _____

19 origin   _____   **20** peculiar   _____

21 courteously _____   **22** theory   _____

23 crisis   _____   **24** endeavour   _____

25 correctly   _____   **26** eat   _____

TEST THREE PAGE 2

DAFFODIL	border planting...............81
	bulb disorder.................219
	container grown............263
	diseases........................214
	fertilizers.......................77
	floral arrangements.......354
	flowering period............137
	indoor...........................279
	lifting............................140
	miniature......................120
	pests.............................202
	planting.........................75
	rockery.........................134
	varieties.......................116
	weed control................181
	wild..............................124

This is part of the index of a gardening book. This section is all about daffodils.

The headings tell you which pages to turn to for information about various aspects of growing daffodils.

Study the index carefully.

Which pages in the book would you refer to, to answer the following queries about daffodils?

27 What can I do to stop weeds growing around them?   Page _____

28 Something is eating the plants. What should I do?   Page _____

29 How many different kinds of daffodils are there?   Page _____

30 What can I give daffodils to make them grow better?   Page _____

31 I have a very small garden. Are there small daffodils suitable for growing in it?   Page _____

32 Where can I find out about daffodils that I have seen growing in forests and out of the way places?   Page _____

33 When can I expect to see my daffodils in bloom?   Page _____

34 I have a steep, stoney place where I grow alpine plants. Would daffodils be suitable there?   Page _____

35 + **36** I bought bulbs, but some of them do not look healthy. Where could I find out about them?   Pages _____ + _____

37 Suggest some ways in which cut flowers could be arranged in vases.   Page _____

Write one word which has the **same meaning** as the words in **bold print**.
Be sure to spell correctly.

Example. The soldiers all obeyed the **person in charge**.   _____officer_____

38 The doctor said he would **come back** tomorrow.   _____

39 The typist **made up her mind** to leave work early.   _____

40 Sam's work was **getting much better**.   _____

41 My sister **looks like** me.   _____

42 The gardener planted cabbages **each year**.   _____

43 The **people watching** left before the end of the match.   _____

44 The **people at the church service** listened intently.   _____

45 The child always arrives **at the right time** at school.   _____

Insert **capital letters**, **commas** and **full stops** where necessary. Write out the sentences.

46 we are travelling to france germany and italy by car

_____

47 i had to read a long boring difficult book

_____

48 tim ran down the road over the bridge across the park and back again

_____

49 jane met a tall dark handsome man

_____

50 there is a beautiful cathedral in canterbury kent.

_____

TEST THREE PAGE 4

TEST FOUR

1,323 NOT OUT

Tom Brown has not missed a day since he started school 7 years ago - a total of 1,323 days. Tom, aged 11, a pupil of Greenfield Primary School said,"I loved school since my first day in the infants. I always seemed to get sick during the holidays. Perhaps it was because I missed the place so much! I missed half a day one time because I had to go to hospital. I fell in the playground and split my head. I was back the next day - four stitches and all!"

Tom's family has been associated with the school for a long time. His father Jim and twin sister, Ann, both joined the school when it opened in 1954. His grandmother, Mrs Edith White had been assistant cook for 14 years before retiring last year. Mr Ron Browne, the headmaster said, " This is the first time in my 26 years in the school that we have had a pupil who has never missed a day. Regular attendance is very important. We try to bring the best out of our pupils and help them reach their full potential.

Thomas Brown has been an asset to this school."

The school, at morning assembly, marked Tom's achievement by presenting him with a gift voucher, an inscribed trophy and a certificate which said, "For excellent attendance, 1st September 1986 to 30th June 1993." As Tom left the school for the last time yesterday, he told our reporter that he hopes to keep up the good attendance in his new school.

Choose the **best word** or **phrase** each time. Underline your answer.

1 The article is from a -   brochure   pamphlet   school magazine   newspaper

2 At school Tom was always -   attentive   present   studious   diligent

3 Tom's attendance was -   regular   infrequent   occasional   inferior

4 On which date was the article published ? _____

5 By what other name is Tom Brown called in the article ? _____

Tom has 3 members of his family connected with the school.
What relation is he to them?

6 _____   **7** _____   **8** _____

9 Is Mrs Edith White his grandmother on his mother's or his father's side of the family ? _____

10 Was Ron Browne in the school when Tom's father was a pupil ? _____

11 How do you know that the headmaster is not a member of Tom's family ? _____

Find words in the article with **similar** meanings to the following.

12 student _____   **13** principal _____

14 infirmary _____   **15** vacations _____

TEST FOUR   PAGE 1

Add a **prefix** to each of the words below to make a new word with the **opposite** meaning.

Use these prefixes.   dis-   in-   un-

e.g.   believe   <u>dis</u> believe.

16. sure   ___ sure.
17. like   ___ like.
18. complete   ___ complete.
19. please   ___ please.
20. correct   ___ correct.
21. able   ___ able.
22. obedient   ___ obedient.
23. official   ___ official.
24. capable   ___ capable.

Insert the words **were** and **where** in the proper places in the sentences below.

25. _____ is my new school uniform ?

26. We _____ very tired after running round the park.

27. There _____ no places _____ the convict could hide.

28. _____ _____ you when I telephoned last night?

29. _____ you pleased to discover the boys _____ home safely ?

30. When we _____ told the dog was lost, Jim said he knew _____ it was.

31. _____ they there _____ we left them ?

32. _____ _____ the books you wanted to read ?

THE DEWEY SYSTEM

In libraries non-fiction books are classified into 10 main groups.
The groups and some of their subject areas are shown below.
Numbers are given to the groups.

000-099	General Works - encyclopaedias, etc.
100-199	Philosophy - Views on life and the universe.
200-299	Religion.
300-399	Social Studies - law, education, occupations, customs etc.
400-499	Language - English, foreign languages and dictionaries.
500-599	Sciences - mathematics, astronomy, chemistry, zoology etc.
600-699	Technology - medicine, business, computers, transport.
700-799	The Arts - photography, painting, music, sports etc.
800-899	Literature - novels, poetry, plays.
900-999	Geography and History.

Study the book titles below and decide between which numbers they are classified.

Title	Number	Title	Number
e.g.		The Ten Commandments	200-299
33 Italian Cities	_____	34 Bassoons	_____
35 Stoats	_____	36 Great Rivers	_____
37 Concorde	_____	38 The Legal System	_____
39 Hinduism	_____	40 The Primary Curriculum	_____
41 Chronic Asthma	_____	42 Winter Verses	_____
43 The Mediterranean	_____	44 Miracles	_____
45 Electronic Ignition	_____	46 Camera Accessories	_____
47 Common French Phrases	_____	48 Roman Soldiers	_____
49 Association Football	_____	50 The Common Cold	_____

TEST FIVE
&
TEST SIX

SCORE: TEST FIVE _____

TEST SIX _____

BOOK OF HOME COOKERY

CHAPTERS.

1. Food Storage
2. Hygiene in the Kitchen
3. Diets
4. Starters
5. Soups
6. Omelettes
7. Snacks
8. Vegetarian Meals
9. Poultry
10. Fish
11. Pastry
12. Cold Desserts
13. European Dishes
14. Indian Meals

*****

In which chapters above would you find the answers to the following questions?

Example - Suggest four suitable sandwich fillings for a child's party.   Chapter __7__

1. What is the recommended temperature for a refrigerator?   Chapter _____

2. Which contains more calories, a baked potato or a sausage roll?   Chapter _____

3. You are having a German pen friend to stay and you want to make her feel at home. What dishes could you prepare?   Chapter _____

4. What is the cooking time for a 10 kg turkey?   Chapter _____

5. Suggest two kinds of fruit that could be served with ice cream.   Chapter _____

6. For how long can eggs be kept fresh in a refrigerator?   Chapter _____

7. Why should food not be left uncovered for long periods?   Chapter _____

8. How much sponge cake is needed to make a trifle for six people?   Chapter _____

9. Name two cold dishes which could be served before a main course.   Chapter _____

10. What are the uses of bleach in the kitchen?   Chapter _____

11. Give three ways in which cabbage, carrots and potatoes can be served together.   Chapter _____

12. You are having a "Continental Night". What kind of dishes could you serve?   Chapter _____

Choose the best words to complete the passage so that it makes sense.
Choose from the words in **bold** type. Circle your chosen words.

13 - 20

LADYBIRDS

Ladybirds are said to be **(some, are, our, their)** favourite insects.

They are liked by gardeners and farmers because they feed on insects **(who, which, what, and)** are harmful to plants. Ladybirds are coloured red or yellow **(also, which, or, and)** have distinctive black spots.

There **(were, are, is, was)** over forty different species of ladybirds.

One kind has only two black spots **(since, because, as, while)** others can have various numbers up to twenty-two. All our ladybirds hibernate **(after, since, during, because)** the winter. In spring and early summer, they lay eggs which hatch **(into, out of, from, to)** grubs. A grub becomes a chrysalis **(then, before, while, after)** becoming a fully grown ladybird.

Complete the following sentences by using the words **to**, **too** and **two** in the proper places.

21 There were _____ many passengers in the _____ buses.

22 If you are going _____ the zoo, may I come _____ ?

23 _____ answer the questions, you must read _____ pages.

24 The _____ boys were stopped on their way _____ the match.

25 The _____ teachers were _____ busy _____ stop.

TEST FIVE PAGE 2

THE DOLPHIN

Moving through the water, a skilled swimmer,
Seemingly taking pride in what he does.
Travelling by an up and down movement of the tail,
He leaps around furiously
And races with a companion,
Chasing after fish,
Hungry for adventure.

They join the school like excited children,
Frolicing about happily without a care in the world.
Suddenly danger looms,
An enemy is near.
They move to another part of the water,
Where they play together,
Safe and content.

Choose the **best word** or **phrase** each time. Underline your answers.

26 The poem makes me feel that dolphins are
    aggressive   playful   nervous   fierce

27 The poet believes that dolphins are
    always racing   continually on the move

    unhappy most of the time   slow movers in water

28 Taking pride in what he does means
    swimming about all day   taking care about what he does

    being safe and content   feeling good about himself

Give **three verbs** from the poem which describe how a dolphin moves.

29 _____ **30** _____ **31** _____

Find words in the poem which mean:

32 Expert at something   _____

33 An exciting event   _____

34 Peril, hazard, risk   _____

35 Springs, bounds, vaults   _____

36 A friend or partner   _____

37 Unexpectedly, without warning   _____

FACT OR OPINION

Decide whether each statement below is a **FACT (F)** or an **OPINION (O)**.
Write **F** or **O** on the answer line.

38 There is no water in a desert. _____

39 Sussex is a county in England. _____

40 Potatoes need to be cooked in salt. _____

41 Spectacles make people look clever. _____

42 Computers do calculations very quickly. _____

43 The invention of the wheel was man's greatest achievement. _____

Insert **capital letters**, **full stops**, **question marks** and **exclamation marks** where necessary.
Write out the sentences.

44 when does the next bus leave

_____

45 hurry up doctor thompson

_____

46 may i go to madame tussaud's on the 5th july

_____

47 how long will mrs roberts stay on saturday

_____

48 get off the grass

_____

49 has christopher won at last

_____

50 get out of here now

_____

TEST SIX

This is taken from the back cover of a book. Study it and answer the questions below.

GARDEN SAFARI
Written and illustrated by Roger Lawn.
Photographed by Arthur Click.

"Garden Safari" takes you on an exciting journey through the average suburban garden.
Marvel at the delicacy of a spider's web. Admire the beauty of our common butterflies.
Wonder at the strength of an ant.
The book is beautifully illustrated with coloured photographs and line drawings.
Clear and concise explanations are given throughout the book by
award winning naturalist Roger Lawn.
This book is a must for those with or without a garden.

£6.99   Published by Pattern Press.

---

1 "Garden Safari" is about one of the following. Underline your answer.
gardening   unexplored regions   nature   jungles

2 In which section of a library would "Garden Safari" be found ?
Literature   Languages   Religion   Science

3 How many people produced pictures for the book? _____

Two adjectives, two verbs and two nouns from the cover are printed below.
Decide what each word is and underline your answer.

4 web   Adjective   Verb   Noun   **7** coloured   Adjective   Verb   Noun

5 common   Adjective   Verb   Noun   **8** admire   Adjective   Verb   Noun

6 illustrated Adjective   Verb   Noun   **9** journey   Adjective   Verb   Noun

The dictionary meaning of a Safari is a hunting expedition.
Match the following dictionary meanings to words from the cover.

Dictionary meaning   **Word from cover**

10 A piece of land for growing flowers etc.   _____

11 An expert on animals or plants.   _____

12 A prize.   _____

13 To think highly of.   _____

14 Explained through pictures.   _____

15 Loveliness, good looks.   _____

TEST SIX PAGE 1

Complete the sentences below with **adverbs**. Choose from the list. Use each adverb only once.

attentively   proudly   fluently   patiently
angrily   accidentally   frequently   leisurely
nervously   generously

16 The old man _____ crossed the busy road.

17 Peter _____ shared his packed lunch with Susan.

18 The audience waited _____ for the show to start.

19 The travellers protested _____ about the delay.

20 Stephen spoke _____ about his book collection.

21 Jill listened _____ to the teacher.

22 The hungry birds _____ search for worms in my garden.

23 On holiday, Janet spoke _____ in French.

24 Mark _____ fell over the boxes.

25 The holiday-makers strolled _____ along the beach.

Underline the **correct word** in each sentence.

26 I was given an enormous (**piece, peace**) of birthday cake.

27 The children enjoyed going to the school (**fair, fare**).

28 The crimson rose had a beautiful (**scent, sent**).

29 Are you (**allowed, aloud**) to go to the cinema tomorrow ?

30 We had no problem with the (**sale, sail**) of the bicycle.

31 There was a serious (**leek, leak**) from the pipe.

32 The (**peal, peel**) of the bell sounded down the valley.

33 My friend lives on the top (**story, storey**).

34 The patient was (**weak, week**) after the operation.

35 I could not (**bare, bear**) to watch them leave.

Information on the subjects below is contained in the encyclopaedias.
Decide which volumes should contain the information and give the volume numbers.

| ENCYCLOPAEDIA A-Bu 1 | ENCYCLOPAEDIA By-Di 2 | ENCYCLOPAEDIA Do-G 3 | ENCYCLOPAEDIA H-Ke 4 | ENCYCLOPAEDIA Ki-Mo 5 | ENCYCLOPAEDIA Mu-Ot 6 | ENCYCLOPAEDIA Ou-Re 7 | ENCYCLOPAEDIA Rh-Su 8 | ENCYCLOPAEDIA Sw-Vi 9 | ENCYCLOPAEDIA Vo-Z 10 |

e.g. icebergs Volume __4__

36 hamsters Volume _____

37 minerals Volume _____

38 leather Volume _____

39 viaduct Volume _____

40 binoculars Volume _____

Which **two** volumes may contain information on each of the following subjects?

41 + **42** Chamber Music Volumes _____ + _____

43 + **44** Roman Baths Volumes _____ + _____

45 + **46** Tower of London Volumes _____ + _____

47 + **48** Oak Trees Volumes _____ + _____

49 + **50** Great Deserts of Africa Volumes _____ + _____

TEST SIX PAGE 3

TEST SEVEN
&
TEST EIGHT

SCORE: TEST SEVEN _____

TEST EIGHT _____

TEST SEVEN

A Gardening Surprise.

"Stephen," his mother said, "you really will have to dig over the garden." Reluctantly he rose from his chair. The rugby on Channel 4 would have to wait. Slowly he walked to the disorganised garage. It took him ten minutes to find a spade. He turned on a tap, washed and scraped the caked clay from the spade.

Slowly he dug at the wet and heavy clay. Ten minutes passed and the fruits of his labours showed little reward. The work was hard and laborious. He pressed hard on the spade with his foot and "clunk," it came to an abrupt halt.

Slowly, meticulously he prised up the large stone and lifted it to the edge of the garden and returned to his digging. Ten more minutes passed and the spade stopped with a hollow thud. "Oh no, not another stone!" he said to himself. He knelt down and removed the soil with his bare hands to expose a rusting box. "Mum," he screamed, "I've found a box! Come out here now!" Quickly he scraped the soil away to reveal an engraved top. He dug deeper and eventually lifted the box on to the surface.
"Look," he said, "it's padlocked." Lifting his spade, he struck the padlock one short, sharp blow - the box sprang open to reveal.................

Choose the **best word** or **phrase** each time. Underline your answers.

1 Reluctantly means -   quickly   happily   unwillingly   slowly

2 Abrupt means -   sudden   slow   long   early

3 Caked clay means -   baked clay   dried clay   boiled clay   heavy clay

4 Fruits of his labours means -   nuts and raisins   the outcome of working
member of the Labour Party   apples on a tree

Write **one word**, from the passage, that proves that each of the following is true.

5 The box was made of metal -   _____

6 The garage was untidy -   _____

7 The box had writing on it -   _____

Read the passage carefully and decide if the following statements are **true, false** or **you cannot tell**. Underline your answer.

8 The man is married.   True   false   I cannot tell

9 The man plays rugby.   True   false   I cannot tell

10 The garden was dry.   True   false   I cannot tell

Choose the best words to complete the passage so that it makes sense.
Choose from the words in **bold type**. Circle one word in each group.

INSULATION

It is very (**obvious, important, exceptional, worth**) to insulate homes to prevent the loss of (**draughts, heat, pets, noise**). Heat can be lost through many parts of a house and this not only (**keeps, wastes, costs, leaks**) heat and energy but adds to our fuel bills. The amount of fuel used can be reduced by (**keeping, insulating, insulation, closing**) the home properly.

(**No, Most, All, Warm**) heat is lost through walls and insulating these can save up to £80 per year on a family's (**energy, water, rates, food**) costs. Insulating walls can be expensive and is a specialised job which should be undertaken by (**keen, expensive, professional, punctual**) workmen. Wherever possible the loft of a house should also be insulated to further (**keep, maintain, reduce, help**) heat loss.

Punctuate the following sentences with **inverted commas** etc.
Rewrite the sentences on the lines.

19. this is the way to do it explained the teacher

20. lesley whispered i think she is asleep

21. i know where you are jane said

22. how much have you left asked tom

23. i ran all the way said laura because of the rain

24. when you were out said lynne catherine phoned

PHYSIOTHERAPY

Physiotherapy is a very varied and interesting career. Students require "A" levels to enrol on a course of study at university. The course includes anatomy, physiology, psychology and physics. On qualifying they are known as Chartered Physiotherapists. Physiotherapists work in hospitals, special schools, health centres, sports clinics and private practices.

Physiotherapy is based on how the body works and physiotherapists use this knowledge to treat injury and disease. They treat many different groups of people - from newborn babies, to Olympic athletes, to frail and elderly people. Many different treatment techniques are used. Some of these include massage, exercise, heat treatment, treatment in water (hydrotherapy) and relaxation techniques.

A very important part of a physiotherapist's job is to give advice on the prevention of injury. Physiotherapists therefore not only treat the condition but give patients advice on preventing the problem from happening again. Many people treated by physiotherapists have long term crippling diseases such as cerebral palsy, multiple sclerosis, Parkinson's disease and spina bifida. Physiotherapists help these people to cope with their handicaps by adopting positions and practising exercises that will help them remain mobile and healthy for as long as possible.

Physiotherapy can be physically very hard work but it is also very rewarding. No matter what the age or condition of a patient, a Chartered Physiotherapist will be able to help.

25 What qualifications do students need to be accepted for the course? _____

26 On qualifying, what are students known as? _____

27 Which word means to give treatment in water? _____

Choose the **best word** or **phrase** each time. Underline your answer.

28 An important part of the job is to give   techniques   injury   advice   health

29 Physiotherapy is based on   the heart   hydrotherapy
    treatment   how the body works

30 Physiotherapy can be   handicapping   hard and stressful
    wet and cold   hard work and rewarding

Find words in the article with **similar** meanings to each of the following.

31 register, enlist _____   **32** weak _____

33 avoidance _____   **34** able to move _____

HOMONYMS are words that sound the same but are spelt differently and have different meanings.
Underline the correct word in each sentence.

Example.   The (<u>**deer**</u>, **dear**) had antlers.

35 The postman hurried (**past, passed**) the barking dog.

36 The bride walked up the (**isle, aisle**).

37 Have you the (**reigns, reins**) for the horses ?"

38 The (**profit, prophet**) on selling the bicycle was £10.

39 The chimney smoked because the (**flew, flue**) needed cleaning.

40 The train was (**stationery, stationary**) at the platform.

41 The horse's (**main, mane**) flew in the wind.

42 It never rains but it (**pours, pores**).

COMPOUND words are words that are formed from two or more smaller words.

Form eight **COMPOUND** words from these two lists of words.
Use one word from each list to make the new word.

Example   **COAST** and **GUARD**   form   **COASTGUARD**.

List one	GO	MAN	RAT	SUP	BULK	IN	SIDE	GENTLE
List two.	AGE	HEAD	PORT	AT	WAYS	MAN	HER	WARDS

43 _____

44 _____

45 _____

46 _____

47 _____

48 _____

49 _____

50 _____

TEST EIGHT

THE ROBIN

The gardener digs, the robin watches,
Never afraid, certainly not timid.
It sits close by, catching small worms and quick moving millipedes,
Its red breast attracting the gardener's eye.

It stops motionless and watches,
Oblivious to its spectator, the robin hops here and there,
Filling its mouth with food for its young.
Then quick as it arrived, it is gone.

Instantly, it returns searching, searching, searching.
The gardener has left to feed and watches from afar.
A cat, a tiger of the garden, stalks the robin,
And pounces, and the robin is gone.

Oh how lucky are its young!

Choose the **best word** or **phrase** each time. Underline your answers.

1	This poem is set in a -	forest	farm	zoo	garden
2	The poet tells us the robin is -	timid	frightened	small	brave
3	Motionless means -	moving	changing	stationary	action
4	A spectator is -	a performer	a feeder	an observer	a friend
5	The robin is stalked by a -	gardener	cat	tiger	dog
6	Pounces means -	snatches	takes off	jumps on	grabs

Which two creatures does the robin catch ?

7 _____   8 _____

9 Why was the robin gathering so much food? _____

10 Which word tells us that the robin returned quickly? _____

11 Why did the gardener leave? _____

12 Which word tells us that he was not close by? _____

13 Which phrase tells us that the cat did not catch the robin? _____

The gardener and the robin both did the same three things. Give two of them.

14 _____   15 _____

Put the eight sentences below into the correct order to make a little story.

Write 1 beside the first sentence, 2 beside the second one and so on.
Number 2 has been done for you.

Sentence order.

"I must have a puncture," he thought.   _____2_____

16 He changed the wheels over and tightened the nuts.   _____

17 A motorist heard a hissing noise.   _____

18 He opened the car door and got out to look.   _____

19 Finally he put the tools away and drove on.   _____

20 He pulled over to the side of the road.   _____

21 He loosened the nuts on the wheel of the flat tyre.   _____

22 A tyre was flat so he took the spare wheel out of the boot.   _____

Rewrite the **underlined words** in their shortened (contracted) form.

Example. <u>I have</u> a dog   _____I've_____

23 <u>They are</u> coming soon.   _____

24 <u>I shall</u> eat it.   _____

25 <u>He will</u> be busy today.   _____

26 I <u>will not</u> go to bed.   _____

27 <u>We have</u> found it.   _____

28 <u>I would</u> come if I could.   _____

29 <u>You are</u> very tired.   _____

30 <u>Who have</u> you brought?   _____

PRONOUNS are words that are used to replace nouns.
Write **PRONOUNS** in place of the underlined words below.

Example. Paul had a ball and threw **the ball**. _____it_____

31) That car belongs to me. It is <u>my car</u>. _____

32) Those boats belong to them. They are <u>their boats</u>. _____

33) Fred and Mike said, "<u>Fred and Mike</u> are going to the zoo." _____

34) Tom said, "The game made <u>Tom</u> tired." _____

35) Stephen has two dogs and he adores <u>the two dogs</u>. _____

36) I have found a cat and I think it is <u>your cat</u>. _____

37) I am sure it was Sarah. I would know <u>Sarah</u> if I saw her. _____

38) Alan promised Brian and Jane that he would feed the birds for <u>Brian and Jane</u>. _____

39) Alice and her mother baked a cake. <u>Alice and her mother</u> made a mess. _____

40) Peter washed the car and <u>the car</u> was clean. _____

Use a **suffix** each time in the sentences below to complete the words in capital letters.
Choose from the following   -less   -able   -ant

Example. The climbers knew it was HOPE<u>less</u> to continue.

41) A person who assists is an ASSIST_____

42) We were able to move the table because it was PORT_____

43) We could not find the toy. Our search was FRUIT_____

44) A person who serves is a SERV_____

45) The man was not CAP_____ of lifting the stone.

46) Since the boys could not understand English it was POINT_____ to continue talking.

47) The carpet was very hard wearing and DUR_____

48) He was sorry for what he had done and was REPENT_____

49) The boy had been in trouble and so he was not GUILT_____

50) The excuse was so bad that it was LAUGH_____

TEST NINE
&
TEST TEN

SCORE: TEST NINE _____

TEST TEN _____

TEST NINE

15 High Street,
Anytown.
22. 6. 93.

Dear Mr. Jones,

Thank you for your letter, dated 18th June, which I received yesterday. I am very sorry to hear that you were dissatisfied with your recent holiday in Spain and also with the treatment that you received from our representative there. Please note that the alleged attitude of our employee is currently being investigated. Please let me try to answer your four queries one by one.
Firstly, your stolen camera is not the responsibility of our company. It should be covered by your insurance policy, provided that you informed local police regarding the theft.
Secondly, the broken shower unit in your bathroom was checked by a local plumber and found to be in perfect working order.
Your third complaint regarding the choice of main courses for your evening meal appears accurate. As you state in your letter, our brochure does say that you would have a choice of four main courses. We apologise that this was not the case on every evening and accordingly, we enclose a cheque for £25 by way of an apology.
Your final complaint regarding your two hour delay on the return flight is unfortunate. I am sure you will accept that it is the responsibility of the airline concerned and not of Getaway Tours. I hope that these responses will help to answer your queries and that you will see fit to travel with us again.

Yours sincerely,
A. Mann.
Customer Services Manager.

Read the statements below and decide whether each one is **TRUE, FALSE**, or you **CANNOT TELL**. Write **TRUE, FALSE**, or **I CANNOT TELL** for your answers.

1. The person complaining had been in Spain.
2. Mr. Mann was making the complaint.
3. Mr. Mann received the letter on the 17th June.
4. The letter from Mr. Jones was handwritten.
5. A cheque for £25 was paid in compensation.
6. The local police were told about the stolen camera.
7. Mr. Jones tried to fix the shower.
8. A choice of chicken, fish, steak and pizza was offered each evening.
9. Getaway Tours promised four main courses.
10. Getaway Tours sent a plumber from England to check the broken shower.
11. The return flight was delayed because of fog.
12. Mr Jones never travelled with Getaway Tours again.

Choose the **best words** or **phrases** to complete the passage so that it makes sense.
Choose from the words in **bold** type.

Circle **one** word or phrase in each group.

13 - 18

SHERPAS

The Sherpa people who live in the mountainous country of Nepal are sometimes known as the **(gateway, gatekeepers, doorway, entrance)** of the Himalayas. Many Sherpas work as porters who **(wash, buy, sell, carry)** equipment on mountain expeditions. The work of a Sherpa can be extremely hazardous and at **(times, once, last, least)** forty-three Sherpas have died while working in the Himalayas. The extreme cold in the mountains **(have, did, has, is)** caused Sherpas to lose fingers due to **(heat, accidents, frost-bite, high altitude)**. Probably the most **(healthy, liked, famous, talked)** Sherpa is Tenzing Norgay who was with Edmund Hillary, the first person to climb Mount Everest.

Use a form of the **verb** on the left to put each sentence into the **past tense**.

Example.   **LEAVE**   They **LEFT** early to attend school.

19 SING   The children _____ in the school choir.

20 DRINK   The cat _____ from the saucer.

21 GO   The girls _____ on the swings.

22 CATCH   The passengers _____ the wrong bus.

23 DO   The boy _____ his homework.

24 TAKE   We _____ sandwiches on the picnic.

25 MEET   After school the boys all _____ at Sam's house.

Read this back cover of a book and answer the questions which follow.

TROPICAL FISH
By Mr. A. Trout

The perfect introductory book for the young enthusiast.
Chapters on setting up a tropical fish tank, care of fish,
breeding tropical fish and much, much more.
The book contains 112 coloured photographs taken by the author in the
habitat of the fish.

Books by the same author.

Fins and Gills	ISBN 1 873385 66 8
Fresh Water Game	ISBN 1 873385 66 6
Life In The Sea	ISBN 1 873385 66 4
Falcons in Captivity	ISBN 1 873385 66 2

Which word or phrase means the **same** or **almost the same** as each of the following words or phrases from the book cover? Underline your answers.

26. perfect – new / ideal / big / first
27. enthusiast – angler / person / devotee / fisherman
28. habitat – river / ocean / natural home / place
29. setting up – establishing / abolishing / keeping / retaining
30. breeding – catching / keeping / producing / giving food to
31. in captivity – in the wild / flying freely / in confinement / released

32. Who wrote the book? _____

33. Who took the photographs? _____

34. What is the title of the book which is not about fish? _____

35. What sort of creature is book ISBN 1 873385 66 2 about? _____

36. What is the title of book ISBN 1 873385 66 4? _____

37. Why are all the author's books listed on the back cover?

When two words are joined together and shortened with an apostrophe they become known as a **contraction**. Decide what the two original words were in the following contractions. Write them on the answer lines.

Example.   I wonder who's in.   who   is

38 **It's** been raining all day.
39 **You're** in trouble now.
40 When **I've** finished I will go out.
41 I hope **she'll** be on time.
42 We **aren't** going until Friday.
43 **I'd** rather stay at home.
44 You **shan't** go to the park.

Rewrite these sentences and insert **all the necessary punctuation**.

45 its said that leaves turn brown in october

46 the flowers are at their best in june remarked michael

47 danger threatens as the light fades said the reporter

48 ive bought apples pears peaches and bananas said norman

49 im going into town said paul but the bus is late

50 theyre coming exclaimed sandra hurry up peter

TEST TEN

 A typist was asked to copy this list but made **10 mistakes**.
Find the mistakes in the typist's copy and put a circle around each one.

Original copy

SURNAME	CHRISTIAN NAME	AGE	CITY,TOWN OF BIRTH	OCCUPATION
Collins	Paul J.	24	Cardiff	Electrician
Clarke	Eric	18	London	Student
Morgan	Samuel T.	37	New York	Cab driver
Smyth	Sandra P.	52	Edinburgh	Housewife
Loanne	Michael W.	11	Bristol	School child
Sloan	Peter	78	Belfast	Retired
Stewart	Mary E.	39	Dublin	Teacher

Typist's copy.

SURNAME	CHRISTIAN NAME	AGE	CITY,TOWN OFF BIRTH	OCUPATION
Collins	Paul J.	24	Cardiff	Electrician
Clark	Eric	24	London	Student
Morgan	Samuel T.	37	New York	Bus driver
Smith	Sandra P.	52	Edinburgh	Housewife
Loanne	Michael W.	11	Bristol	School child
Sloan	Pete	78	Belfast	Retired
Stewart	Mary	89	Dublin	Teecher

Add a **prefix** to each of the words below to make a new word with the **opposite** meaning.

Use these prefixes. **mis- im- ir-**

Example   fortune   **mis** fortune

11. understand   _____understand
12. regular   _____regular
13. behave   _____behave
14. possible   _____possible
15. replaceable   _____replaceable
16. mature   _____mature
17. responsible   _____responsible
18. guided   _____guided
19. patient   _____patient
20. pronounce   _____pronounce

Form **adjectives** from the words in **bold print**.
Write the **adjectives** in the spaces. Be sure to spell correctly.

Example.   **CLOUD**   The <u>**CLOUDY**</u>   weather ruined the holiday.

21 MUD   There were _____ footprints all over the carpet.

22 NOISE   _____ neighbours are not popular.

23 HEALTH   Everyone should lead a _____ life style.

24 FAVOUR   The child's _____ toy was left behind.

25 MARVEL   We had a _____ time at the circus.

26 VICTORY   The crowd cheered the _____ team.

27 SENSE   Fred gave a _____ answer to the question.

28 COMIC   The _____ story made everyone laugh.

Join each pair of sentences by using **conjunctions**. Choose from the following.

WHO   UNTIL   IF   SO   WHICH   ALTHOUGH

You may have to leave words out sometimes. Write the new sentence on the line.

Example.   The boy saw the dog.   It had frightened him earlier.
The boy saw the dog **which** had frightened him earlier.

29 We cannot go to the cinema. We have not enough money.

30 Peter sat in the car. His father changed the wheel.

31 Sarah had finished all her work. She went out to play.

32 I will take you. You behave yourself.

33 Anne found a purse. It had money in it.

34 Bob has an uncle. He lives in France.

35 We will all stay here. The weather improves.

TEST TEN PAGE 2

The following is an extract from the classified advertisements in a local newspaper. Study it carefully and then answer the questions that follow.

CAR SAFETY SEAT, suit 2-4 years. £15 - Tel (1111) 242424	BRASS FIRE IRONS, 80 years old. Ideal gift with Christmas next week. £75 - Call 75, Reed St.	COMPLETE COFFEE MAKER - boxed, never used, unwanted gift. £35 Tel (2222) 444888
VELVET CURTAINS, Dark red. Suit large bay windows. £45 - Call 16, Anyway Lane after 6pm	EARTHENWARE JUG 3 feet high, suit small garden. £5.	WASHING MACHINE £35 ono. Needs repairs. Contact Box 62
SMALL QUILT £10. Ideal for single bed. Flowered patern on green background. Tel 656565	SQUARE TABLE 4ft x 4ft White oak £35 ono. Tel (222) 123456	16 " PORTABLE COLOUR T.V. Ideal for child's bedroom. Offers Tel 123123

36 How much is the small quilt ?

37 For what age is the car safety seat suitable ?

38 What is the table made from?

39 How much are the fire irons?

40 What colour are the curtains?

41 What would I want to buy if I telephoned (2222) 444888?

42 Which item does not have an asking price ?

43 Which words tell you that the washing machine does not work?

44 Why is the coffee maker for sale?

45 In which month was the paper published?

46 How many items are for sale ?

47 How many advertisements give a telephone number ?

48 Which item can only be enquired about in the evening?

49 A word is wrongly spelt in one of the advertisements. Spell the word correctly.

50 Why would it be difficult to buy the earthenware jug?

ANSWERS

TEST 1

1	discount
2	requested
3-5	Any three from 3,4,5,6,7,8.
6-8	Any three from 1,2,9,10
9	1
10	10
11	2
12	4
13	those
14	best
15	since
16	possible
17	direct
18	its
19	patiently
20	loitered
21	knowledge
22	optimist
23	primitive
24	dispute
25	prominent
26	humane
27	temporary
28	potential
29	Marco Polo
30	Roald Amundsen
31	48
32	David Livingstone
33	4
34	2
35	Not sure of date of birth
36	May not be the exact date.
37	1912
38	1909
39	James Cook
40	After Queen Victoria
41	5
42	3
43	2
44	4
45	1
46	because *
47	although*
48	until*
49	but*
50	because*

*Other answers may be correct.

TEST 2

1	warm and friendly
2	sad
3	cars
4	hazardous
5	in peril
6	children
7	lollipop man is poet's grandad.
8	swiftly
9	sad or blue
10	never
11	friendly
12	luckiest
13	boys
14	children
15	sheep
16	boxes
17	wolves
18	geese
19	potatoes
20	soldiers
21	deer
22	wives
23	chiefs
24	shelves
25	heroes
26	oxen
27	their,there
28	their,their
29	there,their
30	their,their
31	their,there
32	there,their
33	there,there
34	F
35	O
36	O
37	F
38	F
39	O
40	piano
41	piccolo
42	trombone
43	trumpet
44	viola
45	violin
46	My name is Jimmy Jones and I live in Bristol.
47	We went to London to visit Buckingham Palace.
48	My favourite television programme is Blue Peter.
49	The 26th December is Boxing Day.
50	My Uncle Philip took me to see the film Home Alone.

TEST 3		TEST 4		TEST 5	
1	residual current circuit breaker	1	newspaper	1	1
2	to protect eyes	2	present	2	3
3	easily ignited/prone to combustion	3	regular	3	13
4	try to fix/repair it.	4	1/7/93	4	9
5	to avoid sparks	5	Thomas	5	12
6	mixture	6	son *	6	1
7	ignition	7	nephew *	7	1 or 2
8	sandpaper	8	grandson *	8	12
9	open windows	9	mother's	9	4
10	E55	10	no	10	2
11	Ideally	11	spelt BrownE	11	8
12	easy	12	pupil	12	13
13	tight	13	headmaster	13	our
14	essential	14	hospital	14	which
15	included	15	holidays	15	and
16	are	16	unsure	16	are
17	fearful	17	dislike/unlike	17	while
18	stubborn	18	incomplete	18	during
19	beginning	19	displease	19	into
20	strange	20	incorrect	20	before
21	mannerly	21	unable	21	too, two
22	idea	22	disobedient	22	to, too
23	emergency	23	unofficial	23	to, two
24	try	24	incapable	24	two, to
25	accurately	25	where	25	two, too, to
26	devour	26	were	26	playful
27	181	27	were, where	27	continually on the move
28	202	28	where, were	28	feeling good about himself
29	116	29	were, were	29-31	Any three from leaps, races, chasing, frolicing
30	77	30	were, where		
31	120	31	were, where	32	skilled
32	124	32	where, were	33	adventure
33	137	33	900-999	34	danger
34	134	34	700-799	35	leaps
35-36	214 and 219	35	500-599	36	companion
37	354	36	900-999	37	suddenly
38	return *	37	600-699	38	O
39	decided *	38	300-399	39	F
40	improving *	39	200-299	40	O
41	resembles *	40	300-399	41	O
42	annually *	41	600-699	42	F
43	spectators *	42	800-899	43	O
44	congregation *	43	900-999	44	When does the next bus leave?
45	punctually *	44	200-299	45	Hurry up Doctor Thompson!
46	We are travelling to France, Germany and Italy by car.	45	600-699	46	May I go to Madame Tussaud's on the 5th July ?
		46	700-799		
47	I had to read a long, boring, difficult book.	47	400-499	47	How long will Mrs Roberts stay on Saturday ?
48	Tim ran down the road, over the bridge, across the park and back again.	48	900-999		
		49	700-799	48	Get off the grass !
49	Jane met a tall, dark, handsome man.	50	600-699	49	Has Christopher won at last ?
50	There is a beautiful cathedral in Canterbury, Kent.	*In any order.		50	Get out of here now!

* Other answers may also be correct.

TEST 6

1	nature
2	science
3	2
4	noun
5	adjective
6	verb
7	adjective
8	verb
9	noun
10	garden
11	naturalist
12	award
13	admire
14	illustrated
15	beauty
16	nervously
17	generously
18	patiently
19	angrily
20	proudly
21	attentively
22	frequently
23	fluently
24	accidentally
25	leisurely
26	piece
27	fair
28	scent
29	allowed
30	sale
31	leak
32	peal
33	storey
34	weak
35	bear
36	4
37	5
38	5
39	9
40	1
41-42	2 and 6
43-44	8 and 1
45-46	5 and 9
47-48	6 and 9
49-50	1 and 2

TEST 7

1	unwillingly
2	sudden
3	dried clay
4	the outcome of working
5	rusting
6	disorganised
7	engraved
8	I cannot tell
9	I cannot tell
10	false
11	important
12	heat
13	wastes
14	insulating
15	Most
16	energy
17	professional
18	reduce
19	"This is the way to do it," explained the teacher.
20	Lesley whispered, "I think she is asleep."
21	"I know where you are," Jane said.
22	"How much have you left?" asked Tom.
23	"I ran all the way," said Laura, "because of the rain."
24	"When you were out," said Lynne, "Catherine phoned."
25	A levels
26	Chartered Physiotherapists.
27	hydrotherapy
28	advice
29	how the body works
30	hard work and rewarding
31	enrol
32	frail
33	prevention
34	mobile
35	past
36	aisle
37	reins
38	profit
39	flue
40	stationary
41	mane
42	pours
43	goat*
44	manage*
45	rather*
46	support*
47	bulkhead*
48	inwards*
49	gentleman*
50	sideways*

* In any order.

TEST 8

1	garden
2	brave
3	stationary
4	an observer
5	cat
6	jumps on
7	millipedes*
8	worms*
9	for its young
10	instantly
11	to feed (eat)
12	afar
13	and the robin is gone / Oh how lucky are its young
14 & 15	any two from:- watching, feeding, went away
16	7
17	1
18	4
19	8
20	3
21	6
22	5
23	They're
24	I'll
25	He'll
26	won't
27	We've
28	I'd
29	You're
30	Who've
31	mine
32	theirs
33	We
34	me
35	them
36	yours
37	her
38	them
39	They
40	it
41	assistANT
42	portABLE
43	fruitLESS
44	servANT
45	capABLE
46	pointLESS
47	durABLE
48	repentANT
49	guiltLESS
50	laughABLE

*In any order

TEST 9

1. true
2. false
3. false
4. I cannot tell
5. true
6. I cannot tell
7. I cannot tell
8. false
9. true
10. false
11. I cannot tell
12. I cannot tell
13. gatekeepers
14. carry
15. least
16. has
17. frost-bite
18. famous
19. sang
20. drank
21. went
22. caught
23. did
24. took
25. met
26. ideal
27. devotee
28. natural home
29. establishing
30. producing
31. in confinement
32. Mr.A.Trout
33. Mr.A.Trout
34. Falcons in Captivity.
35. falcons(birds)
36. Life In The Sea.
37. to advertise/sell other books.*
38. It has
39. You are
40. I have
41. she will
42. are not
43. I would
44. shall not
45. It's said that leaves turn brown in October.
46. "The flowers are at their best in June," remarked Michael.
47. "Danger threatens as the light fades," said the reporter.
48. "I've bought apples,pears,peaches and bananas," said Norman.
49. "I'm going into town," said Paul,"but the bus is late."
50. "They're coming!" exclaimed Sandra."Hurry up Peter!"

*Or similar answer.

TEST 10

1. Clark has E missing.
2. Smith spelt with an i.
3. r missing from Peter.
4. E missing after Mary.
5. Eric is 18 not 24.
6. Mary is 39 not 89.
7. OF spelt OFF.
8. OCCUPATION spelt OCUPATION.
9. BUS instead of CAB driver.
10. TEECHER instead of TEACHER..
11. MIS understand
12. IR regular
13. MIS behave.
14. IM possible
15. IR replaceable
16. IM mature
17. IR responsible
18. MIS guided
19. IM patient
20. MIS pronounce
21. muddy
22. noisy
23. healthy
24. favourite
25. marvellous
26. victorious
27. sensible
28. comical
29. We cannot go to the cinema IF we have not enough money.*
30. Peter sat in the car UNTIL his father changed the wheel.*
31. Sarah had finished all her work SO she went out to play.*
32. I will take you IF you behave yourself.*
33. Anne found a purse WHICH had money in it.*
34. Bob has an uncle WHO lives in France.*
35. We will all stay here UNTIL the weather improves.
36. £10
37. 2-4 years
38. white oak
39. £75
40. dark red
41. coffee maker
42. portable T.V.
43. needs repairs
44. unwanted gift
45. December
46. 9
47. 5
48. velvet curtains
49. pattern
50. no phone number or contact address.

* Other answers may also be correct.

ANSWERS PAGE 4
PUBLISHED BY LEARNING TOGETHER   TELEPHONE   (0232) 402086/425852